Giraffes

Victoria Blakemore

Copyright info/picture credits

Cover, martina paier/AdobeStock; Page 3, Pexels/Pixabay; Page 5, HowardWilks/Pixabay; Page 7, Scubatss/Pixabay; Page 9, Katrina Brown/AdobeStock; Pages 10-11, Iuliia Sokolovska/AdobeStock; Page 13, Vladimir Wrangel/AdobeStock; Page 15, WiseTraveller/Pixabay; Page 17, Alexas_Fotos/Pixabay; Page 19, HowardWilks/Pixabay; Page 21, anujohanna/Pixabay; Page 23; MagdalenaPaluchowska/AdobeStock; Page 25, tpsdave/Pixabay; Page 27, Alexas_Fotos/Pixabay; Page 29, TechPhotoGal/Pixabay; Page 31, markjordahl/Pixabay; Page 33, martina paier/AdobeStock

Table of Contents

What Are Giraffes?

Giraffes are tall mammals. They are known for their long necks and brown spots.

There are four main kinds of giraffes. They differ in the color of their coats, their size, and where they live.

A giraffe's spots are like human fingerprints. Each giraffe has a **unique** pattern.

Size

Giraffes are the tallest animals on Earth. They can be up to nineteen feet tall.

Giraffe necks are about six feet long. That is as tall as some adult humans!

A giraffe's neck has the

same number of **vertebrae** in

their necks as humans do.

Physical Characteristics

Giraffe legs are very long and strong. If a **predator** attacks, one kick from a giraffe can stop it.

Giraffes have two horns on their head. These are called "ossicones." They help male giraffes if they get in a fight.

Their spotted skin works as **camouflage**. It helps them blend in with the trees and grasses.

Habitat

Giraffes are found in savannas, grasslands, and woodlands.

They live in areas with lots of tall trees so they have enough food.

Range

Giraffes are only found on the continent of Africa.

They are found in parts of central, eastern, and southern Africa.

Diet

Giraffes are **herbivores**, which means that they eat only plants.

Acacia tree leaves make up most of a giraffe's diet. The thick skin on a giraffe's tongue protects it from acacia thorns.

Giraffe tongues are dark purple
in color. This keeps them from
getting sunburned. They can be
up to twenty inches long.

Giraffes get much of their water from eating leaves. They can go several days without drinking.

To get a drink, a giraffe must spread it's front legs and bend over. It can be dangerous if a predator is nearby.

Communication

Giraffes are usually very quiet animals. They are rarely heard by humans.

The sounds they make are very low. Humans are not able to hear many of their sounds.

Giraffes are sometimes heard snorting, grunting, or humming. 17

Movement

Giraffes have very long legs.

This allows them to run up to 35

miles per hour for short periods

of time.

They need to be able to run

fast to stay safe from

predators.

Giraffes may have to stretch their

necks to reach leaves in tall trees.

Giraffe Calves

Giraffes may have one or two calves. Their calves are about 6 feet tall when they are born.

Calves are able to walk within an hour of being born. They are able to run within about 10 hours.

Giraffe mothers are very

protective of their calves.

Herd Life

Giraffes are very social animals. They live together in groups called herds. Most herds have between ten and twelve giraffes.

Giraffes usually separate into herds of male giraffes and herds of females and calves.

Giraffes are free to move

from one herd to the next.

Herds may change often.

Helping Out

Giraffe mothers work together to keep calves safe from predators.

Calves that are old enough spend much of the day together. The giraffe mothers take turns watching them.

The other mothers use that time

to find food.

Life Span

Most giraffes in the wild live between 20 and 25 years.

Calves are targets for predators and many do not survive. Adults are not as likely to be caught by predators as calves.

Giraffes are fully grown when they are between five and seven years old.

Population

Giraffes are not **endangered**, but their populations are getting smaller. They are listed as **vulnerable**, which means they may become endangered.

There are believed to be about 97,000 left in the wild.

In 1999, there were over 130,000

giraffes in the wild.

Helping Giraffes

Giraffes are often hunted for their coat. Their habitats are being destroyed as people build roads and buildings.

Wildlife preserves have been built to help protect giraffes in the wild.

Giraffes are also protected

by laws in many countries.

People are not supposed

to hunt them.

Some wildlife groups are

trying to teach people

about the threats giraffes

face. They hope that

people will help if they

know about the problem.

Glossary

Camouflage: using color to blend in to the surroundings

Endangered: at risk of becoming extinct

Herbivore: an animal that eats plants

Predator: an animal that eats other animals

Protective: keeping something

safe from harm

Unique: different, special

Vertebrae: small bones that

protect the spine

Vulnerable: an animal that is

likely to become endangered

About the Author

Victoria Blakemore is a first grade

teacher in Southwest Florida with a

passion for reading.

You can visit her at

www.elementaryexplorers.com

Also in This Series

Also in This Series

Lyla

CPSIA information can be obtained
at www.ICGtesting.com
Printed in the USA
BVHW091007250122
627122BV00010B/436

9 781947 439023